I Am Wonderfully Me: Positive Affirmations for Me!
Volume 1

Photographs and script Copyright © 2012 by Audrey Tait
Reprinted in 2017 in paperback

All rights reserved.
No part of this book may be reproduced, stored in a retrieval system,
transmitted in any form or by any means,
electronic, photocopying, mechanical, recording, photographing or otherwise,
without the written permission of the author and the publisher.

Library and Archives Canada Cataloguing in Publication

Tait, Audrey, 1959-, author, photographer
I am wonderfully me : positive affirmations for me / photography and script by
Audrey Tait, MS.

Title from cover.
ISBN 978-0-9878856-0-9 (v. 1 : hardback).--ISBN 978-0-9878856-4-7 (v. 1 : paperback).--
ISBN 978-0-9878856-3-0 (v. 1 : kindle).--ISBN 978-0-9952326-5-5 (v. 1 : EPUB)

1. Nature--Pictorial works. 2. Affirmations. I. Title.

BF697.5.S47T35 2012   158.1   C2011-908709-X
                                                    C2013-900149-2

Published in Canada by
Inspirational Insights Counselling, Inc.
Suite 120 B102-5212 48th Street
Red Deer, Alberta Canada T4N 7C3
www.inspirationalinsightscounselling.com

I Am Wonderfully Me: Positive Affirmations for Me!

Volume 1
Photography and Script by Audrey Tait

In life, we are all confronted with difficult situations, from the slightly irritating to the abusive (covert or overt). Then there are the words that people (family, authority figures, and friends) speak to us that limit what we do or what we think we can do. These are the tapes that run in our minds–sometimes for years–keeping us stuck where we currently are, stuck from reaching out, and stuck from trying new things. Perhaps we have lost our hopes and dreams or simply stopped dreaming. This book is about change and reaching out. It's about changing the negative thinking that keeps us stuck. For me, this book was about change and taking calculated risks. It was about taking my camera and going into nature to look for images. It included hiking and backpacking in the backcountry. I have taken all the pictures myself. All pictures are as they were taken. None have been changed or edited or even cropped.

To use this book, please view the pictures and then read the title and descriptions. When you come to the words in Bold, read them and then repeat them to yourself–they are designed to help you replace some of your negative thinking with positive thinking. The idea is to come to the conclusion that I am (You are) worthwhile, lovable, and not a victim or helpless. I am (You are) awesome, beautiful, wonderful, worthwhile, and lovable.

*Dedicated to
the awesome memory of Suzanne.
What an inspiration!
And to those who have helped me on my own
personal journey, especially Kurt, Cory, Pat, and
to my children for learning to be yourself.*

****

"Tait's photos and affirmations will be helpful for people struggling with the negativity and destructive messages that can infiltrate our lives—whether those people are in the recovery and mental health communities or are others simply looking for a way to develop positive thinking. This book is a helpful tool in the journey toward healthier living."
—Patrick Carnes, PhD, author of Facing the Shadows

What Am I (Who Am I)?
That looks like a simple question.
Some are chipmunks and some are squirrels.
Maybe, I do not really know who I am.

The Grand Canyon on a Late Winter Afternoon
It is an awesome, harsh, rough, and beautiful environment.
My childhood may have been harsh or beautiful. It may or may not have given me the ability to grow as I needed.
Regardless, **I can decide to change my life as I choose.**

Bondage

Bondage comes in many forms, including physical, emotional, mental, and spiritual. Bondage may be real or perceived.

I do not need to live in bondage. ***I can choose to live life in freedom.***

A Bad Hair Day
Life does not always develop the way we would like it to.
Things in my life may not have been wonderful. I may not have the tools that I need to do what I want to do.
I can decide to change this if I want to.

The Changing of the Seasons
Change is not always the prettiest or the easiest of things.
I may not look pretty during the process of change. Even so, in the end it will be better for me and those around me.
I choose to change for the better.

Charge!
Something dangerous may be coming my way,
something that I may not suspect until it happens.
There are times in my life when I need to protect myself.
I will learn to set boundaries to protect myself.

Mother and Son

The tender loving care of a mother is special.

When this does not happen, ***I can earn a safe attachment in my relationships with others,*** *an "earned attachment."*

A Frozen Tulip

The snow came after the tulip was ready to burst into full bloom. At times, it may feel like I am frozen or numb.

*At these times, **I can choose to take care of myself, which includes learning to accept and simply experience these feelings.***

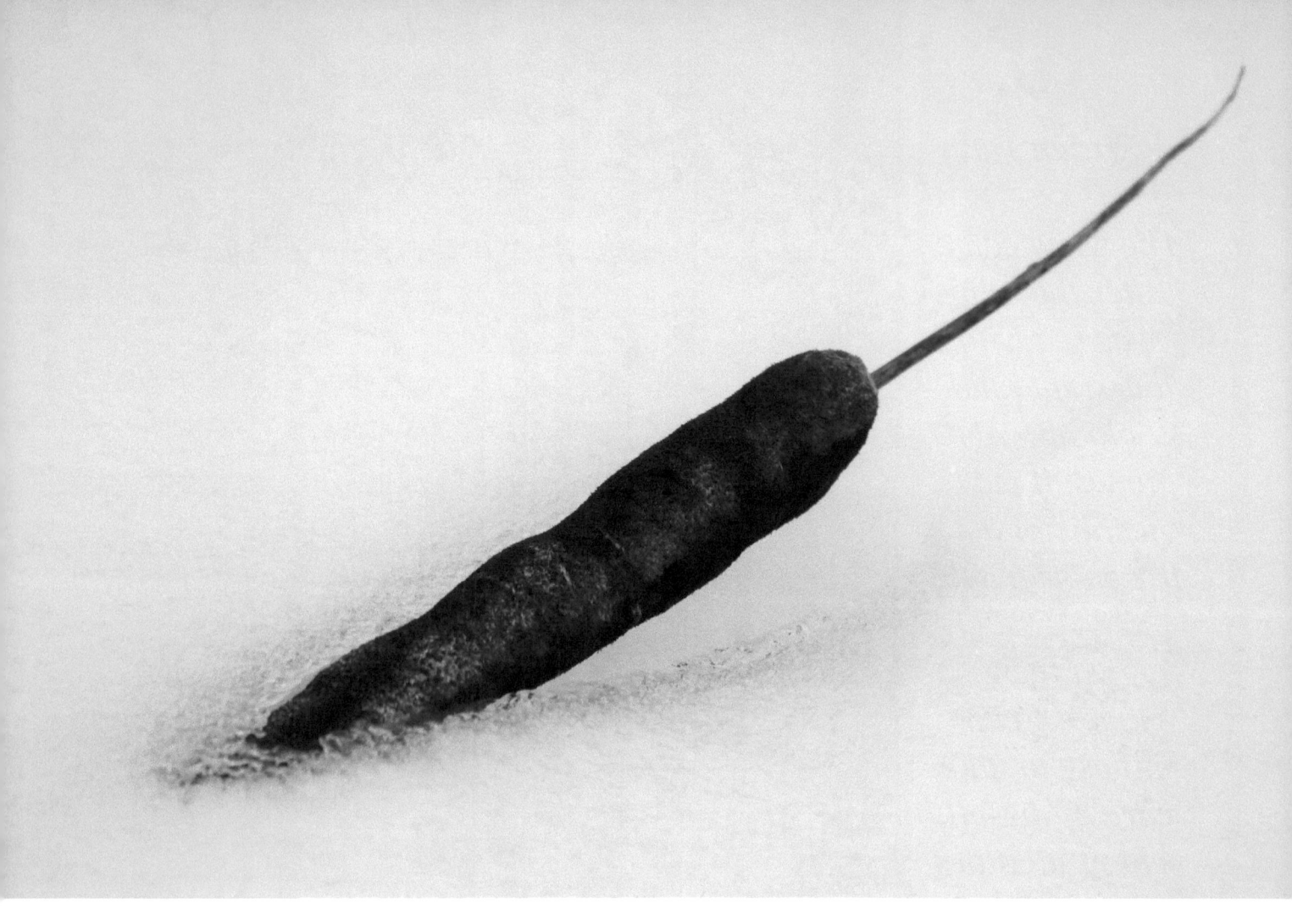

Frozen in the Snow That Turned to Ice
The seasons come and go, just as life sees different seasons–
infancy, childhood, adolescence, and adulthood.
They all present different challenges and require flexibility.
I will learn to be flexible as life changes.

A Social Moment–Just Hanging Out
Even animals are meant to be social. I may be an introvert or an extrovert. Either way, I still need time to socialize.
I will find the time to be social with others
in ways that are healthy for me and comfortable for me.

A Female Elk Finding Food during the Scarcity of Winter

We all have needs (food, water, and a place to sleep) even though we may think we have no needs.

I can meet my own needs. I do not need to rely on others. I can choose to ask for help when I need it.

Eating to Survive

Even when eating, this deer is still looking for the dangers that may lurk nearby.

I will be aware of the dangers that may be around me *even when taking care of myself.*

Partners Each Looking for Food
When I am in a relationship, I am still my own person
and need to look after myself.
I will take care of myself*,*
even when I am in a relationship.

Family
Although we are a family unit,
we are all unique individuals–parent or child.
I will continue to learn to be myself within my family,
an individual within a group.

WHERE DID MY BABY GO in All the Confusion?
When confronted with a human, this wild turkey mother started running around in fast circles to shift the attention away from her young. **When something happens, I can deal with the situation in a way that is safe for everyone.**

Safe over here!

Beauty in Springtime!

Springtime is a time for new beginnings.

Every moment in every day is a time for a new beginning, a chance to do things differently.

Unique–One of a Kind

Tulips come in many different shapes, sizes, and colors. Each one is unique.

I am different from others; ***I am unique in my own way.***

An Elk Enjoying the New Grass in the Spring of the Year

It is easier for an elk to find food to eat in the spring of the year than in the winter.

When my life is a little easier, ***I will spend the extra time relaxing.***

A Moose Taking a Break from Eating

While eating, animals take breaks to look around and see what is going on.

When I eat, I can take breaks. *I can look around and enjoy what is going on in my surroundings.*

A Blue Clematis with the Afternoon Sun Shining on It
The sun highlights the beauty of this flower. Others reveal the beauty in my life by their positive comments.
I will listen to positive comments from others *and let them shine in my soul.*

Glacier Lily Covered with the Morning Rain
Rain is a refreshing element in nature.
Whenever things are difficult for me, I can choose to do something that refreshes my soul.
One way I can refresh my soul is through deep breathing.

A Bighorn Sheep

When looking closely at this sheep, I see he is looking back at me. It even looks as if he is smiling with a couple of his teeth showing.

When I am communicating with others, **I can look them in the eye and give them a smile.**

Two Bighorn Sheep Resting

There are times when one needs to rest from the tasks of life; in other words, needs to just hang out.

*I will listen to my body for signs of needing rest and **I will give myself permission to rest when needed.***

Close-Up

*I am the
sum
of all
my parts—
everything.*

**I can
take care
of all
my parts,**
*even the ones
that I do not
like very much.
Every part
has
a unique
purpose
in my
WHOLENESS.*

A Personal Shield

Even nature and flowers have ways to protect themselves from danger in their surroundings.

I must protect myself from danger*; however, I do not need to isolate myself or let the possibility of danger overwhelm me.*

A Black Bear with Brown Fur

This was a young bear exhibiting strange behavior, like putting his head inside a car.

In the past, I may have done strange or unhealthy things.
Today, I choose healthy behaviors for myself.

A Black Bear with Black Fur

This bear was more mature and looked after his own needs.

Maturity is about loving myself and looking after myself. *Then, maybe, I will be able to help others.*

A Close-Up View

A close-up view really lets one see most everything.

Letting others close to me may be uncomfortable because they will see who I really am.
I can set my own boundaries and let those who are trustworthy be close to me.

Arnica in the Spring Mountain Landscape

The arnica is just part of the landscape.

I can be myself in a group of friends *and still be aware of the environment around me.*

A Beaver Lodge
Homes come in all different shapes and sizes.
Homes are places of protection.
I can make my home a place of protection for myself.
It is the atmosphere that counts!

A Very Curious Beaver
This was a very curious beaver who really checked me out.
Curiosity is a good thing.
I choose to be curious about what is happening in my life.

Beauty in a Group
This was an interesting group of flowers.
Each individual flower is distinct
within the group of flowers from the same plant.
I can be an individual within a group.

Common, Simple, and Beautiful
This common flower that blooms in the fall is exquisite.
I may be very common. That does not mean
that I am lacking in beauty.
I am exquisite!

A Brilliant Evening in the Sun

This doe took the time while eating to look and listen for danger.

***I can take the time to look and listen for danger** before I react!*

A Mother Mountain Goat and Her Young

Scared by human traffic, the pair start up the long path to higher ground.

I will stay close to the people in my life who are safe for me.

A Thistle Reflecting the Dew in the Morning Sun
The flower is inspiring; the thistle part sparkles, yet it is prepared to hurt. I can concentrate on the beauty of the flower or I can concentrate on the thorns of the thistle.
I choose to concentrate on the beautiful things in life.

*Venus's Slipper
or
Calypso*

An amazing flower that is hard to describe!

I want to be an amazing person and **I choose to be an amazing person.**

The Reflection of the Sunset on the Beach
A time of quiet and peace—one of those moments when my soul just goes, Mmmmmm.
I can take the time to feel the atmosphere around me, to feel the peace of being me.

The Reflection of the Sunset on the Mountain
The sun produced an awesome reflection on the mountain. The mountain did nothing for this beauty but receive it. There are times in my life when I do nothing for something beautiful except receive it. **I will be a willing receiver.**

An Almost Open, Hairy Prairie Crocus against the Cloudy Sky

To get this perspective of the crocus against the sky, one has to get down on the ground.

I choose to find the best perspective for each situation in my life.

A Rare Find–
a
Pink Prairie
Crocus

This crocus
is
a rare
find
with
a rare
beauty.

I am
a rare
beauty
that I
choose
to let myself
and
others see.

Columbine
This flower has a lot of interesting structure that contributes to its beauty. I have a lot of structure in my life from the past. Some of it may not be beautiful.
I choose to create a beautiful structure in my life.

What Am I?
This bud has a lot of texture.
As time goes on, its beauty will unfold.
As I change,
my beauty will start to unfold *as well.*

A Twin Grizzly Cub
Even at such a young age,
this cub has learned to watch for danger.
Today, I choose to be alert for
signs of danger.

A Baby Humpback and Its Mother
Babies need a lot of loving attention, nurturance, and protection to grow. Now, regardless of my age,
I will be loving to myself, nurture myself, and protect myself *so that I can continue to grow and change.*

Triplets

Here are three flowers on the same cactus. Thistles, like cacti, have prickly parts that hurt to touch.

I can look at the positive or negative things in life.
I choose to dwell on the positive things in life.

A Pink Trillium
An endangered flower that is protected by some laws.
I may have been in dangerous situations in the past; some of them may have been of my own choosing. ***Now, I choose to remove myself from dangerous situations.***

Sunbathing on the Beach in the Early Autumn
This butterfly was soaking in the warmth of the sun.
One way to soak up the warm energy in my life is to soak up the positive comments of others.
I choose to listen to others' positive comments about me.

The Sun Reflecting Off of the Morning Dew
Hmmm—what is this?
It is a reminder of becoming older with white hair.
Today, I choose to live life to the fullest,
so when I get older, I will have no regrets.

A Different Shape of a Prairie Rose; It Has Allowed Its Leaves to Curl Backward

There may be times in my life when I feel like I am moving backward instead of forward.

I choose to create a long-term vision for my life that will help me move forward.

A Prairie Rose Bud about to Burst Forth into Bloom
This bud has a lot of potential.
When I decide to make changes in my life,
I am like a bud about to burst open.
I have a lot of potential.

Fungus on the Tree Stump
*Fungus loves to grow on old tree stumps. So it is with us—
sometimes choices leave us covered with fungus.
Today, **I choose a positive path** that will help me remove the
fungus growing on me.*

The Pathway into the Woods

The pathway takes us places we have not been before. It allows us time to explore.

Today, I choose to take the time to explore something new in my life. *It may be a new path, a new place to go, a new hobby, or a new friendship.*

A Harebell–a Beautiful Flower

This is not a perfect picture. There is a spot on the camera that shows up on the top of the flower. I may not look picture-perfect when I do something, but I am still "good enough" to do it. **I do not need to avoid doing it.**

A Blue Moon

*A
blue moon
does not
happen
very
often.
Some things
are rare
in life.*

**I will
treasure
the
rare
moments
in
my life.**

A Baby White-Tailed Deer Still with His White Spots

This white-tailed fawn and a baby mule deer were being raised together by their mothers.

My family may look different; *it may be a chosen family.*

A Baby Elk

This baby was being raised by a large group of elk. It was hard to tell who the mother and father were.

My family may be small or large; whatever its size, it is still my family.

A Perfect White Waterlily
This flower was found in the mouth of a stream
where the water was slowly moving toward the lake.
It was a peaceful place, a good place to be.
I choose to spend time in places that are peaceful.

"Stunning," as One Person Said

Being stunning, handsome, or beautiful can be seen in many different ways. It can be seen from an inward or an outward perspective.

I am a stunning person!

What Are You Doing?
I do not think that I can trust you.
When I cannot trust you,
I will set my boundaries close to my soul
so as to protect myself.

Over the Grand Canyon, about to Land
The depths may be great below me
when I feel like I am in free fall.
I can help to break my fall and soften the landing
by concentrating on what I need to do to make it easier.

*A Pink Prairie Rose
in the
Evening Sun
Creating Its
Own Shadow*

This flower is protecting its more delicate parts with its own shadow from the sun.

When it's necessary, ***I can also protect my more delicate parts.***

A Western Anemone on a Mountain Slope Creating Its Own Shadow in the Evening Sun

Just as I can protect my delicate parts, so can I let my strong parts shine.

I choose to let my talents and my abilities shine.

Moraine Lake in July before the Sun Descends behind the Mountains
What a breathtaking picture!
I can sit back and enjoy the beauty of nature
that surrounds me.

Spirit Island on Maligne Lake
The spirit of this place is incredible!
It takes time to really experience the spirit or feeling of a place.
In my life, I choose to look for the feeling of places.
This means **I will take the time to feel.**

Hanging on for Dear Life

There may be times when I feel like I am just hanging on for dear life. **This, too, will pass.** *The flower above speaks of future hope.*

I will look for the hope for the future *that will take me through this rough spot.*

Sheltered–a Much-Needed Place of Safety
At times when I feel like I need shelter,
I will find the people who can help shelter me.
I will set my boundaries where they need to be
so that I am sheltered.

The Evening Sun on the Rocks beside the Colorado River at the Bottom of the Grand Canyon

It was an awesome place to be!

The peace of the moment is a treasure to remember.
Each day, I will look for moments to treasure in my life.

The Top of the Grand Canyon from the Bottom of the Canyon a Mile Below

It was a long walk with a 35-pound backpack, including enough water for the trip.

To follow my dreams, I am willing to make the extra effort and spend the time to get there.

The Evening Sun on Two Mountain Lady's Slippers

These were two of many flowers from the same plant–siblings from the same family.

The sun shines from a different perspective on each flower.
Parents treat each child differently.

Clinging on for Dear Life

This baby was chased by his/her mother out of her home/nest. For hours afterward, the baby clung to this tree, not moving one inch. Talk about being scared!

*When I am scared, **I will allow myself the time to rest and recover.***

Singing on a Cold Winter Day
Circumstances in life can be really tough, like cold weather. Yet, like the birds, I do not need to worry about life. When the going gets tough, ***I can sing a happy song and if I do not know how to sing a happy song at first, I can learn to.***

After the Snowstorm

There are times in life when it is impossible to avoid the storms or stress that exist around me.

After each storm, ***I choose to return to a peaceful state of mind.***

Relatives
Everyone is different.
I can be myself
and be different from the rest of my family,
relatives, or friends!

Tiger Lily

All the parts make this a whole flower. Even the sepal and the pistil are necessary parts.

Even my sex organs are part of my body and they help make me whole. They are not dirty or ugly. **They are to be treated with respect and care.**

Sharing the Gulf of Mexico Beach in the Late Autumn
In the past, sharing has not always been a part of life or of human history.
Today, things are slowly changing–it takes a long time.
In a healthy way, I can choose to share with others.

Friends Hanging Out Together
They may be different kinds of birds,
yet they can hang out together.
My friends may be different from me,
yet I can still hang out with them and be myself.

Watch Out! I Am Observing You
Danger always lurks around me, so I can be on alert for it.
In situations that are potentially dangerous,
I can rest and yet be prepared for it.
I do not need to overreact to the possibility of danger.

A Bullfrog
The bullfrog is hard to see unless you really look for it or see its movements. I do not need to allow myself to seem invisible to those around me.
I choose to let others know that I am in their presence.

A Close-Up of a Prairie Rose Producing Its Own Shadows

This looks like a flower within a flower.

*I have made some ugly shadows in the past; now, **I choose to create new shadows that are healthier for me.***

Water—an Amazing Magnifier
Water helps one see more detail.
I can magnify the positive perspective in any situation
and also remember to keep my boundaries
in place to protect myself.

Yes, I Can Live in the Grand Canyon
The desert of the canyon still offers enough for my survival.
There may be times when I do not have all that I want, yet
I still have what I need and
I can survive.

Eating—What Is That?
I am not sure what the squirrel is eating.
At times, I am not sure what I am seeing, hearing, tasting,
smelling, feeling, or doing. This is when
I need to stop and contemplate what I need to do next.

A Red-Winged Blackbird
While landing, this bird found that this dried growth was not stable enough to hold him.
He had to keep hopping until he found a secure footing.
Every day, I can find a secure footing for myself.

Standing Firm
While gradually walking out into the water,
all of the birds except for one took to flight.
I can stand firm when everyone else leaves me.
I can believe in myself.

The Stillness of the Evening Allows for an
Awesome Reflection
Mmmmmmm.
Words cannot describe this one!
I want to create an awesomeness in my life.

The Calm (Serenity) of Early Spring
Taking time to create serenity is very important!
In the past, I may have lived in chaos or rigidity.
Today, I choose to create times of calmness and serenity in my life.

Sunrise over the Grand Canyon
At the beginning of each new day, I get a fresh start—
a fresh start to do things differently.
Today,
I choose to do things differently.

Sunset over the Ocean
The end of the day is a time for reflection.
I will take the time at the end of my day or at the end of a journey
to compassionately reflect on what I did really well and what I would choose to improve.

Working Together
The geese work together in flight, taking turns in the lead position. I also cannot do it alone.
I need to work with others in a safe environment and allow them to help me change.

THE SKY IS THE LIMIT!

A New Beginning! It is Yours for the Choosing!

About the Author

Audrey Tait has a love of photography and has a master's degree in Addiction Counseling and a bachelor's degree in Dietetics. She is a Canadian Certified Counsellor; Certified Sex Addiction Therapist, candidate; Certified Multiple Addiction Therapist, candidate; and Registered Dietitian, Alberta, Canada. In addition, she is a member of the Canadian Counselling and Psychotherapy Association; College of Dietitians of Alberta; and the Alpha Chi Honors Society. She has specialized training in trauma, character, and developmental issues along with cognitive therapy. She is owner/president of Inspirational Insights Counselling, Inc., where therapy is offered to those seeking a deeper meaning in life.

www.inspirationalinsightcounselling.com

Other Books Available

I Am Wonderfully Me: Positive Affirmations for Me! Volume 2

I Am Wonderfully Me: Positive Affirmations for Me! Volume 3

Reflective Meditations: Understanding My Trauma

Reflective Meditations: Healing My Trauma

Reflective Meditations: Letting Go—Forgiveness

Reflective Meditations: Understanding My Authentic Self

Reflective Meditations: Believing in Myself

Reflective Meditations: Understanding My Boundaries

Reflective Meditations: Loving Myself

www.ingramcontent.com/pod-product-compliance
Lightning Source LLC
Chambersburg PA
CBHW041121300426
44112CB00003B/50